A True Story

fatty legs

10TH ANNIVERSARY EDITION

A True Story

fatty legs

10TH ANNIVERSARY EDITION

Christy JORDAN-FENTON *&*
Margaret-Olemaun POKIAK-FENTON

Artwork by Liz Amini-Holmes

annick press
toronto · berkeley

ONTARIO ARTS COUNCIL
CONSEIL DES ARTS DE L'ONTARIO
an Ontario government agency
un organisme du gouvernement de l'Ontario

Library and Archives Canada Cataloguing in Publication

Title: Fatty legs : a true story / Christy Jordan-Fenton & Margaret-Olemaun Pokiak-Fenton ; artwork by Liz Amini-Holmes.
Names: Jordan-Fenton, Christy, author. | Pokiak-Fenton, Margaret-Olemaun, 1936- author. | Amini-Holmes, Liz, artist.
Description: 10th anniversary edition.
Identifiers: Canadiana (print) 20190167440 | Canadiana (ebook) 20190167890 | ISBN 9781773213507 (softcover) | ISBN 9781773213514 (hardcover) | ISBN 9781773213521 (ebook)
Subjects: LCSH: Pokiak-Fenton, Margaret-Olemaun, 1936-—Childhood and youth—Juvenile literature. | LCSH: Inuit—Biography—Juvenile literature. | CSH: Inuit—Canada—Residential schools—Juvenile literature. | LCGFT: Autobiographies.
Classification: LCC E96.5 J65 2020 | DDC j371.829/9712071—dc23

We acknowledge the support of the Canada Council for the Arts and the Ontario Arts Council, and the participation of the Government of Canada/la participation du gouvernement du Canada for our publishing activities.

FOR MY THREE INSPIRATIONS—Qugyuk, Aklak, and Paniktuaq. I wrote this for you to be proud of who you are and where you come from—a long line of brave, resilient survivors and thrivers. For Olemaun: your courage is unparalleled. Thank you for sharing this journey with me and with the world, and for being your grandchildren's greatest hero. For my Morris Crow/Yellow Thunder family, and for all the survivors and spiritual mentors past and present who have guided me to my own healing and taught me how to carry these stories in a good way. Ni-Kso-Ko-Wa *All My Relations*.

—*Christy*

FOR MY LATE HUSBAND, LYLE, who helped me to work through the many fears I carried with me from residential school. Your love gave me courage. And, for our children, their husbands and wives, and our many grandchildren.

—*Margaret-Olemaun*

A Note on the Right to Silence

THE AUTHORS WOULD LIKE TO ask readers to be mindful of the Right to Silence. While Margaret-Olemaun is open about sharing her experiences at residential school, it is important to stress that many residential school survivors will not wish to talk about or revisit what they experienced. Best practices include respecting their silence. This extends to all experiences of Indigenous trauma. We are overwhelmed by the level of inquisitiveness that has replaced a century and a half of horrific secrecy, but encourage those who want to know more to seek out sources where knowledge has been shared freely, and to accept what is shared on the terms by which it is given.

TABLE OF CONTENTS

Foreword

DEAR READER,

You are about to read a rare story! In your hands (or on your e-reader) is *Fatty Legs*. It is rare because it is written by a Indigenous person and it tells the truth about history and the experience of Olemaun, the little girl in *Fatty Legs*.

Most of the children's books, television shows, movies, and lessons in your schoolbooks do not tell the truth about what happened to Indigenous Peoples when Europeans came onto their homelands several hundred years ago. Most of the stories are biased. That means they show things in favor of one group over another, in a way that is often inaccurate and unfair.

People who are not Indigenous have been writing biased stories about Indigenous people for hundreds of years. You have probably read a lot of books like that already. In many schools, children in third and fourth grade read *Little House on the Prairie*. This series of books makes it seem like Laura Ingalls and her family were doing a good thing, settling America, but it ignored the fact that the land they were settling on belonged to Indigenous people and their families.

White people did terrible things to Indigenous people when they came to what they called the "New World." To the Indigenous Peoples who were here, it wasn't a "new" world at all! We had been on our lands for thousands of years, building towns and establishing trading networks. At first, Europeans took Indigenous land and forced many Indigenous Peoples onto reserves (more commonly called reservations in the United States)*. In the 1800s and 1900s, they took Indigenous children away from their families. The children were taken to schools that tried to make them give up their language and culture. Olemaun went to one of these schools.

Today, more Indigenous people are writing stories about their lives and history. *Fatty Legs* is one of those books. I am glad that it was written, and I am glad that you are reading about Olemaun. If you want to read more books by Indigenous writers, take a look at *The Birchbark House* by Louise Erdrich. She's Ojibwe. When you get to middle school, you can read *Rain Is Not My Indian Name* by Cynthia Leitich Smith. She's Muscogee Creek, and her stories are about Muscogee Creek girls and their families. And when you are in high school, read *This Place: 150 Years Retold*. It is an eye-opening graphic novel anthology featuring work by many Indigenous authors and artists.

Government leaders in the United States and Canada wanted Indigenous people to stop being who we are, but we are persistent! Our lives as Indigenous people mean a lot to us. People like Olemaun care about their lives as Indigenous people. They want their children and grandchildren to have stories that tell the truth, and they want others to know those truths as well. I hope that you tell your friends about Olemaun. I hope you tell them to read her story, and then tell them to look for other books by Indigenous writers who have important stories to tell, too.

Sincerely,
Debbie Reese
Nambé Pueblo
Founder of American Indians in Children's Literature
americanindiansinchildrensliterature.net

---

*from page ix: Many Indigenous nations in Canada and the U.S. were forced into signing treaties with the settler governments that colonized their homelands, which led to their removal or confinement to reserves and reservations. However, in Canada, no treaties were signed after 1923, when Indigenous people were prohibited from hiring lawyers, preventing them from obtaining legal representation to settle land claims. Most nations in the province of B.C., as well as in the north of Canada, and other often outlying territories, did not enter into treaties as a result, and thus continue to occupy unceded (or unsurrendered) territories, though settlers have encroached on and vastly reduced their territory sizes. Margaret-Olemaun's people, the Inuvialuit, reside on unceded territory and have never belonged to reserves. Their land claim was recognized in the Inuvialuit Final Agreement, signed in 1984.

Preface

IT ALL STARTED ON a stretch of gravel during a routine drive to town. That's where I first heard the now famous words, "They used to call me Fatty Legs." There was no predicting where that road was about to lead.

As the grandmother of my children, Margaret is an invaluable knowledge keeper. My children gain their knowledge of what it means to be Inuvialuk through her. From the time they were born, I started bugging Margaret to tell me stories of growing up in the High Arctic, where she traveled by dogsled and schooner and hunted wolves, musk ox, and polar bears. But that day, on that drive, she told me a very different story . . . the story of when she left that world to go to residential school.

That *Fatty Legs* has made such a big impact seems almost unbelievable looking back to when Margaret first shared her 65-year-old secret—the secret of what she did with her stockings. It was 2008, two years before the Truth and Reconciliation Commission began, in a time when most non-Indigenous Canadians had never heard of residential schools. I didn't know if anyone would connect with the experiences of a young girl far from home in such a terrifying place, but I did know that Canada had kept its secret about the residential schools for too long. I also knew that this was the first story an elder had ever told me about residential school where the child retained her agency and determination in the face of unparalleled bullying from adults. She actually claimed a victory over the oppressive nuns! The young Olemaun moved into my heart. Amplifying her voice became an obsession for me. But elder Margaret had other ideas. She said no.

She says, "I didn't want my grandchildren to know I was naughty at one time" for what she did to her stockings. We laugh now that she only gave in because she thought no one would ever read it. But people did read it. Not just in English, but also in French and Korean.

It was more than just the fear of being perceived as naughty. It was embarking on a long journey, after six decades, to fully free her child self from that school. Olemaun was the hero I set out to write about. Margaret has been the hero who has made it possible, recounting her stories in four books, and to a hundred audiences a year, in places as far away from her home in north-eastern BC as Anchorage, Havana, Seattle, and Halifax. A musical production based on *Fatty Legs* has been staged countless times by Xara Women's Choral Theatre, starring Sarain Carson-Fox. She is also featured in the music video for Native American Music Hall of Fame inductee Keith Secola's song, "Say Your Name." She is even recognized by strangers. But it hasn't all been glamor and adventure. It has taken an enormous amount of reconciliation with self, a painful exfoliation of shame, and so much bravery to allow others, myself included, to carry her story alongside her.

Reaching the 10th anniversary of *Fatty Legs*, I realize it has been more than just a childhood story, it has also been the re-emergence of a spirit named Olemaun. When that courageous young girl stepped forward to be heard, she brought healing with her for countless intergenerational survivors who grew up trying to understand the legacy of the residential school system that haunted the adults in our lives. Margaret-Olemaun has encouraged other survivors of the residential school system to share their stories. She has given new Canadians someone to identify with as they navigate between culture shock, assimilation, and the desire to maintain traditions. She's shown children from all walks of life that no matter how hopeless or shamed you feel, you can make it with the strength of your spirit.

To paraphrase Neil Gaiman's words about scary fairy tales, the stories are not important so that children can know dragons exist, but so that they can know they can defeat them. That's what this story is to me. Yes, it is important that we all know such dragons existed and were real, but the universality of Margaret-Olemaun's story is found in how she faced her dragons. She walked into that residential school in Aklavik with exceptional strength of spirit and cleverness, and under the most horrific and powerless circumstances imaginable, she survived. Margaret-Olemaun reminds us to give credit to the strength of Indigenous children and their spiritual fortitude and wit, to honor them, and to hold them up for the very courageous act of surviving. There's a reason why the Raven isn't referred to by a proper name in *Fatty Legs*. The story isn't about the dragons. It's about the heroism of surviving residential school.

My part in Margaret-Olemaun's journey began only as a desire for my children to have no greater hero than their grandmother. My eternal gratitude to all of you who have joined us on this journey, and who now count Margaret-Olemaun as one of your own heroes.

For all of our readers, especially the very young ones, we would both like you to know, no matter what you are going through, no matter how hopeless it seems, though you may not see it now, you are the hero of your own story.

Christy Jordan-Fenton

Olemaun, who was later called Margaret, at home on
Banks Island. Here she stands (on the right) with two of
her younger sisters, Elizabeth and Mabel.

Introduction

MY NAME IS OLEMAUN POKIAK—that's OO-*lee-mawn*—but some of my classmates used to call me "Fatty Legs." They called me that because a wicked nun forced me to wear a pair of red stockings that made my legs look enormous. But I put an end to it. How? Well, I am going to let you in on a secret that I have kept for more than 60 years: the secret of how I made those stockings disappear.

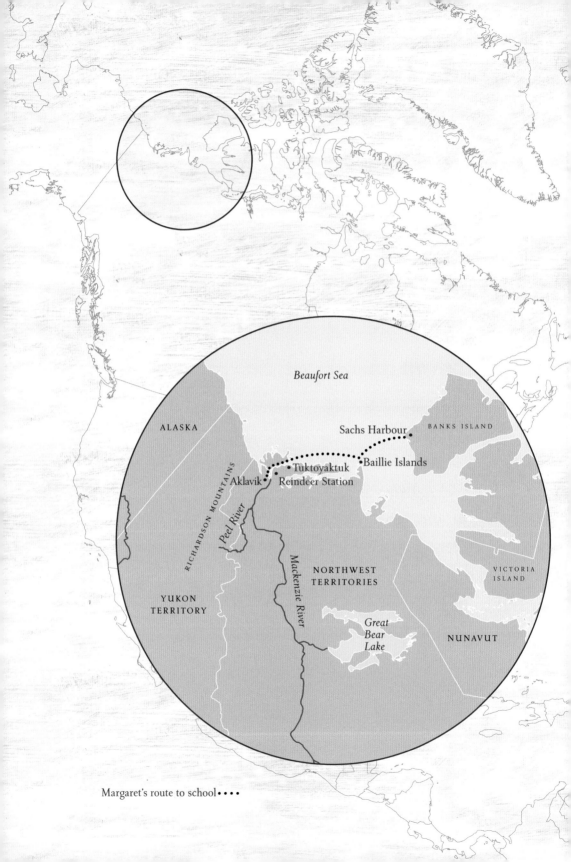

Margaret's route to school •••

Chapter ONE

WHEN I WAS A YOUNG GIRL, outsiders came flitting about the North. They plucked us from our homes on the scattered islands of the Arctic Ocean and carried us back to the nests they called schools, in Aklavik.

Three times I had made the five-day journey to Aklavik with my father, across the open ocean, past Tuktoyaktuk, and through the tangled Mackenzie River delta, to buy supplies. I was mesmerized on each trip by the spectacle of the strange dark-cloaked nuns,

See photo on page 92.

See photo on page 92.

whose tongues flickered with French-Canadian accents, and the pale-skinned priests who had traveled across a different ocean from a far-off land called Belgium. They held the key to the greatest of the outsiders' mysteries—reading.

My older half-sister, Ayouniq, had been plucked before I was born, but we called her "Rosie" after her return. She would tell me nothing about the school tucked away in the maze of the delta, where she had gone for four years, but when I was seven she did read to me from a collection of beautifully colored books my father had given her for Christmas. The stories were precious treasures to be enjoyed in the well-lit, toasty warmth of our smoke-scented tent, as the darkness of winter was constant, and the temperatures outside were cold enough to freeze bare skin in seconds. The books were written in English, so I understood very little of them. I was always left with many unanswered questions.

"What's a rabbit?" I asked Rosie in our language, Inuvialuktun.

"It's like a hare," she told me, lifting her eyes from *Alice's Adventures in Wonderland*.

"Oh. Well, why did Alice follow it down the hole? To hunt it?"

Rosie gave me a funny look. "No, Olemaun. She followed it because she was curious."

I tried to imagine being Alice, as the large cookstove crackled behind me. She was brave to go into that long, dark tunnel, all for curiosity.

"What was it like?"

Rosie looked up from the book again. "What was what like?"

"The outsiders' school."

"I don't know. You ask too many questions," she said. Her face grew dark in the light of the coal oil lamp.

Inuvialuktun: the language of the Inuvialuit, who are the Indigenous Peoples whose traditional territory spans the western Arctic.

She closed the book and looked away.

"It must have been exciting to live with the outsiders."

She shrugged her shoulders and dropped the book on the table.

"But they taught you how to read . . ."

Rosie was silent.

"Please," I begged, tugging at her leg as she got up from the table and slipped on her Mother Hubbard parka.

"They cut our hair because our mothers weren't there to braid it for us."

"I don't need my mother to braid my hair. I can do it myself."

"They'd cut it anyway. They always cut the little ones' hair."

"I'm not that little."

"They don't care. They don't have the patience to wait for you to braid your hair. They want all of your time for chores and for kneeling on your knees to ask forgiveness."

"Oh, well. It's only hair."

"It isn't just your hair, Olemaun. They take everything," she said, slipping her feet inside her kamik.

Mother Hubbard parka (atikluk): the traditional parka worn by Inuit women of the western Arctic.

"Well, can you at least finish reading me the story?"

Rosie gave me an icy look. "You want to know about the school so much, you can go there and learn to read for yourself." She turned, pulled apart the flaps of the tent door, and disappeared through the tunnel in the snow that formed the entrance to our home. I ran after her down the dark corridor, but she was already gone into the pitch-black afternoon of the Arctic winter. She knew that our father would not let me go to school. He had told the outsiders "No" the past four summers they had come for me. Rosie was lucky that her aunt had allowed her to go.

See photo on page 93.

ONE DAY AT THE end of February 1944, when the sun had just begun to return to the sky, my father took me hunting with him. We traveled by dogsled for several hours, until we came to a place where game was plentiful.

"Father," I said when we finally stopped, "can I go to the school this year?"

"No," he said.

kamik/kamak: a type of boot worn by the Inuit. Also called mukluks.

"But you and Rosie both went, and I will be eight in June when the ice melts."

He raised his hand, silencing me, and motioned for me to return to the dogsled. Atop a distant hill stood a wolf, its silhouette stark in the afternoon twilight. My father had it in the sights of his rifle. A shot cracked through the air, killing my chance to convince him.

When he returned to the dogsled with the wolf carcass, his knit brow and hard eyes told me that he was finished discussing the matter. I cringed under the cold flash of defeat, but I was careful not to talk any further about my desire to go to school. Instead, I held it inside all through the long months that followed.

My father rarely spoke of the school and would never tell me of the wonderful things I could learn there. He was a smart man who loved to read, but he put little value in the outsiders' learning compared to the things that our people knew.

But my heart would not give up hope. I climbed the cemetery hill and stared out over the sleeping, stone-still water each day, waiting for the sea to come alive with waves. Sometimes, I brought the book with me,

See photo on page 93.

the one about the girl named Alice who followed the hare-like creature down the burrow. I looked at the pictures and remembered the tea party she had, and how her body had become small and large again. But I still did not know what happened to her at the end of that burrow. Did she catch the hare?

IN LATE MAY, WHEN the sun stood constant watch in the sky and night traversed it only briefly like the shadow of a passing bird's wing, I found my father preparing the hides of animals he had collected from his trapline. I knew the topic was forbidden, but I could not silence my heart another day. I asked him once again to allow me to go to school.

"The outsiders do not teach you how to hunt," he said, pointing his knife at the fox he was about to skin. "They only use your knowledge of making snares for their own profit and send you to gather the animals from *their* traplines. They do not teach you how to cure meat and clean fish so that you can live off of the land. They feed you cabbage soup and

See photo on page 94.

10

porridge. They do not teach you how to make parkas and kamik," he said, eyeing the beautifully crafted Delta braid on my parka and the embroidered, fur-lined boots on my feet. "They make you wear their scratchy outsiders' clothes, which keep out neither the mosquitoes nor the cold. They teach you their songs and dances instead of your own. And they tell you that the spirit inside of you is bad and needs their forgiveness."

I had already learned a lot about hunting, trapping, and curing foods. My friend Agnes, who was 10, had already gone to the school. She told me that the nuns made you sew all of the time. It would not be difficult to learn to sew parkas and kamik if I was used to sewing all of the time. And how could I ever forget our songs and our dances? They were a part of me. But I had once heard the outsiders' beautiful chants resonating from the church in Tuktoyaktuk, and I dreamed of learning to make such music. I would be careful to stay out of trouble, and no one would say I had to kneel and ask forgiveness. They would see that my spirit was good.

Delta braid: a decoration made by cutting patterns from long strips of fabric and layering them on each other; used to decorate Mother Hubbard parkas.

I would be patient, but I would not give up. I would wait and ask my father again.

Time melted away. My eighth birthday came and went. The sea began to wake from its slumber, and I knew it would not be long before the ice broke from the shore and was carried out to be swallowed by the ocean. Soon all of us—my father and the other hunters and trappers, along with their families—would leave our winter home on Banks Island to carry boatloads of pelts to Aklavik. The outsiders had many islands to scour for children during the short summer season, and ours was a long distance from Aklavik. As it was so far for them to travel, it was unlikely that we would be there when they came. My father was my only hope.

One day in late June, I looked up from staring at the book I was so desperate to read and saw that the enormous splintering chunks of ice had left enough of a gap to allow us passage. I slammed the book shut, sped down the hill, and ran along the rocky shore as fast as I could—which was fast, because my legs were muscular and strong. I was determined and ready to ask again.

"Father, Father, please, Father . . . *Pleeease*, can I go to school this year?" I huffed in heavy breaths, darting through the small groups of men who were loading the schooners for the journey.

My father heaved a bale of white fox pelts over the edge of the *North Star*. His answer had not changed: "No."

"Please, please, *pleeease*," I begged. "You can drop me at Aklavik when you go for supplies."

My father paused to swat a mosquito. He looked into my eyes. "You are a stubborn girl," he told me, "and the outsiders do not like stubborn children."

"Please," I said again. "Please."

He crouched to my height. He picked up a rock with one of his hands and held it out to me. "Do you see this rock? It was once jagged and full of sharp, jutting points, but the water of the ocean slapped and slapped at it, carrying away its angles and edges. Now it is nothing but a small pebble. That is what the outsiders will do to you at the school."

"But Father, the water did not change the stone inside the rock. Besides, I am not a rock. I am a girl,

schooner: a type of sailing vessel with masts.   13

I can move. I am not stuck upon the shore for eternity."

"You are a clever one," he said, touching my cheek and then looking down at the book in my hand.

"Does that mean I can go?" My hope blossomed, billowing beneath my parka.

He looked deep into my eyes, the rock held tightly in his fist. "I suppose it is the only way I will hear the end of it."

I turned to run and tell my mother the news, but my father reached for me and pulled me in. He held me in his arms for a long time, the fur of his parka pressed against my face, so that I could hardly breathe. When he finally let go, I did not give him a single moment to change his mind. Even faster than I had run to the shore, I ran back up to my mother, who was in our tent packing up the belongings we would need for the journey.

"Mother, Mother!" I shouted as I rushed through the entrance. "Father says I can go to school this year!"

See photo on page 94.

She did not say a word. Instead, she set my little sister down on a caribou hide, pushed past me out of the tent, and headed straight for him.

I could tell she did not think it was such terrific news.

Chapter TWO

THE SCHOONERS WERE FULL to the gunwales with a winter's worth of pelts for trading. Everything we needed for the trip had been packed from our tents. The men used long poles to pry the boats free of the shore, where they were stored for the winter, and a system of pulleys to pull them back into the water. Planks were laid down to bridge the gap between the shore and the schooners, and we all climbed aboard and prepared for our spring migration.

Stefansson expedition: the Arctic expedition of 1913 to 1916, organized by Vilhjalmur Stefansson, a Canadian explorer of Icelandic descent.

We traveled with six other schooners, each carrying as many as six or seven families. Our schooner was the *North Star*. It was owned by Mr. Carpenter and Mr. Wolki, but had once been part of the famous Stefansson expedition's fleet. We stayed aboard the ships for the entire five-day journey.

See photo on page 95.

Five days may not seem like much, but to me it might as well have been a year. From the first day, I searched for signs that we were nearing the mainland. The voyage across the ocean was fraught with anticipation, and when we finally reached Tuktoyaktuk, I felt both happiness that we had made it that far and sadness that we still had a long way to go. Beyond Tuktoyaktuk, the pingos rose out of the ocean like goose eggs with smashed-in tops. We passed them and entered the mouth of the Mackenzie River. The Richardson Mountains cut into the horizon far off to the southwest, and small, sparse trees lined the shores. We came to Reindeer Station, a settlement of herders, and excitement consumed me. We would soon be heading up the Peel River, the last leg of our journey.

See photo on page 95.

See photo on page 96.

pingos: when ice forms in the ground during winter months, it pushes the surface earth up into small hills, or pingos, which grow bigger year after year. The name pingo comes from the Inuvialuktun word for small hill.

17

Sometime after lunch, on the final day, the noise of children playing reached our ears, and we could see spiraling towers of smoke rising high into the sky from many campfires. A dozen boats as large as whales were tethered to the bank. We had made it! We had reached Aklavik!

After our schooner was secured and a large board was laid over the side of the *North Star*, we children were given permission to go and seek out our friends and cousins, who had also arrived to sell their pelts and stock up on supplies for the year. We made our way down the plank and scrambled up the steep muddy slope to the settlement our own great-grandfather, Old Man Pokiak, had founded as a trading post.

See photo on page 96.

LATER THAT DAY, AFTER my father had sold his winter's catch of furs, my mother came to find me. I was giddy with excitement, knowing what was to come. I tossed the caribou-hide ball I was playing with high into the air, leaving a cluster of children scrambling for it, as I followed my mother to the Hudson's Bay

Hudson's Bay Company: the oldest surviving company in North America, incorporated by a royal charter in 1670. Hunters and trappers traded their pelts there for goods and supplies.

Company. The Hudson's Bay Company was a magical place. They sold everything a person could ever need, from furniture to ladies' dresses, from rifles to candy.

See photo on page 97.

My mother stopped me on the stairs before I could race into the small treasure-packed timber building. She took one of my long braids in her hand. "You know, the nuns will cut your hair. Are you sure you still want to attend the school?"

"Yes," I told her and tried to make my face very serious.

"They will make you work hard. Harder than you do when you help your father."

"I am strong," I said, pushing my shoulders back.

"They will not be kind to you. They are not your family, and they are not like us."

"I will have Agnes. I will be fine. You will see."

My mother sure seemed to know a lot about a place she had never been. I figured she was trying to scare me. Life would be more difficult without me there to help her with the smaller children, and she was likely jealous of my opportunity to learn to read.

"Well then, we had better go in and find you some new stockings to keep your legs warm underneath your uniform."

My mother bought me some strange-smelling soap, a comb to keep my hair neat, a brush for my teeth, and something in a white tube. She also bought me a thick, heavy pair of gray stockings. They were like the kind I had seen the outsiders wear, the kind that pull up above your knees. I wanted to put them on right away, but my mother told me I had to wait. I would not want to soil them before school, because the outsiders loved cleanliness.

As we left the store, I noticed a member of the RCMP relaxing on a chair near the entrance. The Mountie was reading from one of the many richly colored books that crammed a tall column of shelves beside him. How distinguished he looked as he pulled at a pipe, a book in his hand. Soon, I, too, would be able to read.

MY PARENTS DID NOT let me go to school right away. They wanted to keep me until after the athletic games,

RCMP or Mounties: Royal Canadian Mounted Police. Canada's national police force.

which were held on Dominion Day, the first of July—
three whole days after our arrival. July was a festive
time of year for the Inuvialuit of the Inuit peoples, and
the Gwich'in of the Dene Nation. Freed at last from
the ice, the men would bring their families to Aklavik
not only for supplies, but to also compete against each
other in tests of strength. I was disappointed that I

*Dominion Day: Canada's national holiday, now
known as Canada Day, which is celebrated on July 1.*

could not go to school immediately, but I did not often get to see my cousins and enjoyed visiting with them.

On the first day of the games, my father made a balloon for us by blowing up the sac from the throat of a ptarmigan. We chased each other down a long, seemingly endless street, the sound of our feet clomping and thudding against the wooden boardwalk, batting the balloon into the air and stealing it from one another. I caught it and ran. Soon I could no longer hear my sisters and cousins behind me. I had lost them.

I looked up and stopped, forgetting the balloon.

In front of me, at least a dozen children dressed in uniforms crouched in a silty garden, breaking the earth and pulling at roots with small tools. These had to be the naughty children who were made to kneel for forgiveness. Behind them stood two immense wooden buildings, so much larger than our schooner, with rows and rows of windows. I had forgotten how big these buildings were.

This was where I would go to school, but I would not be like these children. I would be good and spend

ptarmigan: white game birds of the grouse family and the official bird of Nunavut, a territory in Canada. Also known as snow chickens.

all of my time inside, learning to read. I batted the balloon from one hand to the other, and turned and ran back to find my cousins and my sisters.

The day after the athletic games began, a boat docked. We watched its passengers file up the beach. They were children with solemn faces, some of them crying. I searched the faces for Agnes, but she was not among them.

See photo on page 97.

"See those children," my mother said to me. "They will be your classmates."

"Why are they crying?" I asked.

"Because they do not want to go to the outsiders' school."

"Don't they know they are going to learn to read?"

"They would rather be with their families than read," my mother said, tightening her lips. Her words stung.

"Now that the other new children are here, it is time for us to take you to the school," my father said, coming up behind us. "Go and gather your things."

MY PARENTS LED ME along the same street I had run down to lose my sisters and cousins, the day before. The buildings came into view. The garden was deserted now.

"Are they both schools?" I asked my father.

"No. Only that one." He pointed at the building on the right. "The other is the hospital where you will be trained when you are old enough. You may be asked to help out there at times."

"Like a nurse? That sounds fun."

My father gave me a look that said he did not think so. "The top floor is where the students sleep. The building is divided into a boys' side and a girls' side, and you will not be allowed to talk with the boys, even if they are your cousins."

The school was beginning to look less inviting. I wondered how I would ever feel safe enough to sleep in such a large place. I was used to staring at the glowing coals of my father's pipe, from where I slept under his bed, until I drifted off. It suddenly sank in. My family would not be staying with me. How would I fall asleep without that smoky red glow?

"The church is in the middle of the dorm rooms, and the classrooms and refectory are below them," he explained.

"What is a refectory?"

"A place where many people eat together."

My mother was silent. She did not say a word until my father had his hand on the big double doors of the school. "It is not too late to change your mind, Olemaun."

Change my mind? I could manage. I would read myself to sleep like Rosie did. I wasn't going to let anything stop me. I couldn't wait to go inside.

My father placed a hand on my shoulder. "You will not be able to return home for a very long time."

"I know," I said, but I didn't.

My eighth birthday had only just passed. I did not yet understand how long a year was. It had not crossed my mind that the same ice that allowed my people to travel only in the brief weeks of summer would keep me from going home. I did not know that an unusually short summer in 1945 would hold me prisoner for a second year with the Sisters, the Fathers, and the Brothers. They were not family; they were like owls and ravens raising wrens.

My father pulled open the door, and I stepped past him. I was inside a school for the first time in my life. All around me was glass and wood. An enormous photograph hung on one of the clean, painted walls. In it, an outsider wore a fancy sash. Medallions like large coins hung from his chest—I would learn later that he was the king of all of the outsiders. They told me he

See photo on page 98.

26

was also my king, but I knew that my family listened to no one but Mr. Carpenter and Mr. Wolki, who owned the *North Star.* The school's smells were unfriendly and harsh against the tender skin of my inner nostrils. I craned my head in every possible direction I could, without moving my feet. It was like someone had enlarged the Hudson's Bay Company by many times and stripped it clean. My eyes darted from wall to wall, trying to take it all in.

An outsider with a hooked nose like a beak came for me, her scraping footsteps echoing through the long, otherwise silent halls. "I am glad you have come to your senses," she told my father in Inuvialuktun. "*You* certainly can't teach her the things she needs to know." She wrapped a dark-cloaked arm around my shoulder and ushered me away, without giving me a chance to say goodbye. I looked back and saw my father wiping tears from my mother's face. I wanted to run to her and tell her that it would be all right, but a priest approached them right then and they walked away with him.

Chapter THREE

I FOLLOWED THE BEAKED NUN up stairs that creaked under my feet to a large room filled with beds. Across the room were seven girls, who had been among the sullen children I had seen earlier. They were standing in a somber line in front of four foul-smelling, wooden stalls along one wall. The outsider pushed me into place at the end of the row, and I nearly gagged from the odor that wafted from the stalls behind us.

Another dark-cloaked nun passed by each girl, eyeing them up and down, one by one. She clutched a large pair of shears. She stopped in front of a small sickly-looking Inuit girl. I knew the girl must be of the Copper Inuit from Victoria Island, because her parka cover was drawn high at the sides, the back hanging low like a beaver's tail, unlike the Mother Hubbard parkas we wore in the west. The girl shrank under the nun's glare. Catching a firm hold on one of the girl's long braids, the nun snipped it off with a clean slice and let

Inuit: a general term for the Inigenous Peoples—including the Inuvialuit and Copper Inuit—who inhabit the Arctic regions of Canada, Greenland, Russia, and the United States. The term "Inuit" has largely replaced "Eskimo."

it fall to the floor. The girl hid her face in her hands as the second braid was cut.

The nun did the same to five other girls, sparing only one older girl, and one of the outsiders' children who was likely a German trapper's daughter. The sound of the shears severing thick black hair drowned out the howls of the disgraced girls.

At last, only I remained. I held my breath. I was large for my age. Surely she would pass over me.

She did not. She stopped directly in front of me. I stepped back from her heavy cross, which nearly struck me in the face, but she reached out and yanked me back by one braid.

"I can fix my own hair," I protested in Inuvialuktun, but she held tight and, with the same motion a bird makes to pull a piece of flesh from a fish, clamped the jaws of the shears down on my braid and severed it. I was horrified. I wasn't a baby. My other braid fell to the floor to meet the first, and I joined the others in their weeping.

There we stood, sobbing in the humiliation of our discarded hair.

A tall Gwich'in girl in a uniform came into the room. She
gave a comforting look to one of
the weeping girls, who I knew to
also be Gwich'in by the wrap-
around moccasins she wore. My

mother had warned me about the Gwich'in. They were
not like us Inuvialuit and did not get along with our
people. The uniformed girl looked at me. A thin, mal-
icious smile crinkled her lips.

I wished they would cut her hair, too.

She was joined by three other braided girls in uniforms. One of the nuns said something to them that I
did not understand. They marched out the door and
returned, moments later, with their arms full. I looked
for Agnes among them, as they scurried between us
passing out the impractical clothes that we were to
wear. They had us exchange our warm, comfortable
kamik and moccasins for outsider-shoes, and issued
each of us a short-sleeved blouse and two pinafores,
one navy blue and one khaki. But the worst were the
scratchy canvas bloomers. They expected us to wear

underwear made out of the same stuff that tents were made with. They knew nothing of living in the North, nor how to dress for it.

The hook-nosed nun shrieked something. I had no idea what she was saying. She held her bony finger out, pointing it directly at me. The floorboards of the dormitory groaned, and I held my breath, scared of what might come next. From a distance, a familiar voice whispered, "Change into the new clothes."

I turned, and there was Agnes. She had come in and joined the other uniformed girls. One of the nuns hurried over to her, a harsh rasp flying from her mouth. I felt bad that Agnes had gotten into trouble for speaking to me, but I was glad she was there. I gave her a hint of a smile and began to dress.

I hated my new clothes. I was much larger than the other girls my age, and the clothes did not fit well. The shoes pinched my feet. The bottoms were hard and stiff. They did not form to the shape of my foot like I was used to, and there was no padding inside of them. The faded, black secondhand stockings were as transparent as walrus intestines and much too small. They did not

Yup'ik: the Inuit who live in western and central Alaska and at the easternmost point of Russia.

reach to the elastic bottoms of my bloomers, so I had no way of holding them up. It was a good thing my mother had bought me my own stockings. I reached into my bag and pulled them out, but the nun snatched them from me with a scaly claw. I stood up straight, hands on my hips, and let out a huff.

"And who do you think you are?" she asked me in my own language.

"I am Olemaun Pokiak," I told her, puffing my chest.

"We use our Christian names here. And we speak English." She narrowed her eyes. "You are Margaret," she said, switching languages.

She could say what she wanted—I knew what my grandfather had named me. It was Olemaun, the same as his Alaskan-Yup'ik mother, and it meant the hard stone that is used to sharpen an ulu. But I could not tell her, because I did not speak nearly enough English. Nor could I do anything about my clothing, though I knew my knees would play peek-a-boo with the cold when I walked, and my toes would freeze as they poked holes through the ends of my onionskin tights. Why would she not just let me wear my own stockings?

ulu: a knife with a rocker-like blade, traditionally used by Inuit women for tasks such as scraping hides, cutting hair, and preparing food.

The nun scuttled to the wall facing the stalls. With one long bony hand, she picked up a cloth from a shelf that was lined with washbasins and made a circular motion with it in front of her face. She pretended to scrub behind her ears and under her armpits. I didn't need a lesson on how to wash my face. I already knew how to do that. What I needed was to learn how to read.

After she finished her class on washing, she opened her mouth and let out a squawk. First, the outsider's daughter took out a tube and a toothbrush from among her belongings. The rest of us did as she did. I placed some paste from the tube on the end of my toothbrush, and stuck it in my mouth. It was worse than a fly's breakfast. I couldn't help but gag and spit it out. The raven-like nun called out "Katherine," and the Gwich'in girl who had smiled when my hair was cut tore the tube from my hand and took it to her. The nun cackled and held the tube up for the other girls to see. The older ones laughed loudly, especially the Gwich'in girl called Katherine. The Gwich'in always thought they were better than us.

A tall slender nun appeared in the doorway. She was pale and seemed to float across the bathroom floor. She turned to the Raven, seeking an explanation for the commotion.

I could hardly take my eyes off her.

The Raven made a gesture from her cheekbone to her jaw, like a man shaving his whiskers. The new girls now laughed, too.

My mother had bought that tube for me. They were not just laughing at me. They were laughing at her. I wanted to tell the nun that it was not funny. My mother could not read. How was she to know that she was buying shaving cream and not toothpaste?

I saw the muscles of the tall nun's beautiful, long neck tense, but she did not laugh. She glided toward me and pulled a small tube from her pocket.

I am not trying that, I thought. *I have had enough of the outsiders' pastes.*

She took a drop from the tube, placed it on her own tongue, and smiled. After rinsing my brush, she put a strip of the paste on it. "Mmm," she said.

I trusted her smile, so I put it in my mouth. It was cool and refreshing like the mints my father had once bought us at the Hudson's Bay Company. As I ran the brush across my teeth, I could see the tall nun in the mirror. She looked like a pale swan, long and elegant. Later, Agnes told me that her name was Sister MacQuillan, and that she was in charge of all of the other nuns. She would be the perfect woman to teach me how to read, but reading, as I discovered, would have to wait.

Once we had finished cleaning ourselves, it was time to clean the school. We were separated into groups. I was lucky: I was put into Agnes's group. We were assigned to clean one of the classrooms. We wiped down the desks, the walls, and the floor with a harsh-smelling liquid that made our eyes water and ate at the skin on our fingers.

After we had dusted, swept, and washed everything, we rubbed wax into the wood floor until it was as smooth and as slick as ice. Agnes and the other girls had fun slipping and sliding around on it, but my stockings were too worn on the bottoms for sliding. I perched myself in one of the small wooden desks to see how it would feel. Letters, like those from Rosie's books, decorated the walls of the classroom. I stared at them, trying to decipher what they might mean.

See photo on page 98.

Suddenly, the girls fell silent. I turned to see why. *WHAP!* A stick came down on the desk I was sitting in. I jumped in my skin. The Raven stood over me, with a look that made it clear she did not approve of me sitting down. I scrambled to my feet. She shoved a dusting cloth in my hand and pointed to the rows and rows of books at the back of the class. The other girls were dismissed to get ready for dinner, but I had to stay.

By the end of my first day, the only books I had touched were the ones I dusted.

I HARDLY SLEPT THAT night. The bed had a rickety frame that creaked every time I took a breath. Each girl's bed was as loud as mine, and the noise filled the vast space of the large room with a disjointed foreign sound, unlike the sleepy rhythmic breathing of my mother, father, and siblings, with whom I had shared a tent since birth. Sobs also carried through the room. My eiderdown blanket was soft, but I missed the musky smell of furry hides, the comforting aroma of smoke drifting through the air, and the darkness of the tent, even in summer. The thin serge curtain above my bed did little to keep the midnight sun from penetrating the huge room. Gathering the blanket off my assigned bed, I crawled underneath it, squinted my eyes, and imagined that my father's pipe was glowing in the distance.

They woke us very early the next morning, but my sleep had been almost as brief as the short-lived darkness. By the time the nuns entered the room, clapping

their hands fiercely, I was dressed and seated on the edge of my bed. I was not about to let another minute stand between me and my chance to learn. However, all I was about to learn was what was to be done with the smelly buckets I had discovered in the stalls, the night before. We called them honey buckets, but there was nothing sweet about a bucket that was used as a toilet. With extreme care, we hauled them down the stairs and across the school yard, where we dumped them in the river. When we returned, we were set to work cleaning the chicken coop. A long time passed before we were herded back upstairs and given a few minutes to attend to our hygiene.

My stomach ached with hunger and my mind ached for knowledge. I could not wait to go to Sister MacQuillan's class and begin reading.

See photo on page 99.

After we were inspected for cleanliness, we were led in single file into a strange room that separated the boys' and girls' dormitories. It was filled with long benches, instead of desks, but there were books placed along them. At last, I would learn to read. Standing at the head of the room was the priest who had taken my parents away the day before. I spotted Sister MacQuillan in the front row, but she did not get up to teach us. Instead, the nuns came around and made us get down on our knees and hang our heads. It seemed like an odd way to learn anything. Agnes saw my confusion and whispered to me in Inuvialuktun, "We are supposed to pray for our souls."

I nodded my head and prayed to start class soon.

My prayers were not answered.

After kneeling, we were taken to eat a breakfast of soggy, bland, mushy oatmeal. Each bowl was sprinkled with a scant teaspoon of brown sugar, which hardly disguised the revolting, tasteless stuff.

42

I wondered how Agnes, who was sitting next to me, could eat it with such enthusiasm.

"You get used to it," she said, shrugging her shoulders.

"Really? So, do we learn to read after breakfast?"

Agnes put down her spoon and turned to face me. Her face was sad and sympathetic. "Oh, no, we will not begin classes until the ice freezes again in the fall."

I stared at her, horror replacing hunger in my belly. My spirit sank like the stockings that slouched around my ankles.

Why had I been so eager to come here? I thought of my sisters and cousins. They were still in Aklavik, nearly within shouting distance. I wanted to yell to them to wake my father and tell him to come and get me so that I could spend the day dancing and watching the games.

"What do we do, until then?" I asked her, fearing the answer.

"We do chores, and we play."

I had spent so many days anticipating the thaw, and now I would spend my days scrubbing, gathering wood, and mending uniforms, impatiently waiting for the freeze.

Chapter FOUR

THE SUMMER TOOK AN eternity to pass, but eventually it did. I was working outside one day when the last of the outsiders' boats returned to Aklavik carrying both freshly plucked children and those they had regathered. We saw them make their way past us, where we knelt in the garden.

"We will start classes tomorrow," Agnes told me. I felt like dancing around the potatoes, but the Raven was watching me, and I didn't dare.

Walking into the classroom the next morning, I stood as straight as I could. I was hoping to impress Sister MacQuillan, but I was in for a shock. The kind nun wasn't there. It was the Raven who hovered behind the large wooden desk, where Sister MacQuillan should have been. How could the Raven be my teacher? The smile shrank from my face as I squeezed into the small desk that she pointed me to. Unfortunately, it was right in front of hers. After all of the other children had been seated, she let out a croak. By now, most of us who were new had become very good at following the cues of the older girls. We had even learned a few phrases of English.

Each of us found a reader inside of our desk. We pulled the books out and set them before us. The Raven rose from her seat, closing in on me, and pointed a yard stick in my direction, motioning for me to stand.

"She wants you to read aloud," whispered Agnes from the seat behind me.

I rose to my feet, but how was I to read? I didn't even know which page to turn to.

See photo on page 99.

The Raven cocked her hip and tapped a foot. *"Welllll?"* she said.

My cheeks felt hot. I looked around me, from child to child. The faces stared back, blank, waiting, as my stockings began to slide down my calves.

The Gwich'in girl raised her hand high into the air.

"Katherine," acknowledged the nun.

She rose and started reading aloud from her own schoolbook.

The Raven raised a wing-like arm, silencing Katherine. She turned back to me and pointed her finger to the ground.

The other children giggled.

"You can sit down now," Agnes said in a soft voice.

How did the Raven expect us to learn without speaking to us in our language, so we could understand?

My first reading lesson had not been what I had anticipated. I was grateful when it was over, and I launched myself from my desk, eager to follow the others outside to play. But the Raven stopped me. She put a brush in my hand and pointed to the colossal chalkboards. I gave her a questioning look. I did not know why she was making me stay to clean them.

She answered with something in English that I did not comprehend, and my older classmates cried with laughter as they left the room.

Later, I stopped Agnes in the hall.

"What did the teacher say that made the others laugh at the end of class?" I asked.

"She said that cleaning the boards should be no problem for you, because you are so tall your stockings won't even stay up."

"She has it in for me. I know she does."

"Who?" asked a lyrical voice in our own language. It was Sister MacQuillan. We had not noticed that we were standing in front of her office.

"No one, Sister," answered Agnes, in English, before tugging me down the hall.

THE RAVEN THOUGHT SHE knew a lot, but she cared more about making us do chores than about teaching us. She said that chores were part of our education. For some reason, she seemed to think that I needed more of an education than the others, and as the weeks went by, I was forever mopping the floors, tidying the recreation room, and emptying the honey buckets. I wasn't sure what she meant to teach me, but I had something to teach her about the spirit of us Inuvialuit.

See photo on page 100.

ONE EVENING IN OCTOBER, after a hard day of the Raven's education, I sat over my bowl of cabbage soup in the long dining hall, watching the other children eat. It was the same food we had been force-fed when we first arrived, and I remembered how many girls had become ill. Those same girls were now lapping it up, because they were starving. It made me angry. How could they expect us to eat this meatless mush? My father's sled dogs would not have licked the bowl it was put in. My stomach hurt, but that night I refused to touch it to my lips.

"Perhaps you need help with your appetite," suggested the Raven as she dropped a soppy wet rag right in my lap. She didn't have to say another word. By now, I knew that she intended for me to wipe down all of the tables.

I looked to Katherine and the other Gwich'in girls. They were like a flock of open-mouthed hatchlings, giggling at me.

"If I had a pocket of stones, I would shoo you with a storm of pebbles," I said, and pushed the rag to the floor.

That Raven swooped down and clutched my dress in her claw. "This is no place for a willful child," she hissed.

I jerked back, knocking my bowl over.

The mush oozed down the Raven's dark habit. This time the hatchlings were laughing at her. She raised her claw at me and I crouched to avoid the blow. Then Sister MacQuillan glided between us, the Swan protecting me with her gentle wing.

The Raven fixed her sharp little eyes on me for a long moment before scuttling off to clean herself up.

The refectory had long since been deserted by the time I made it to the last table. A dark shadow grew in the doorway. It was the Raven. "You seem to require a little more education!" she whispered.

I knew I was in for trouble.

Chapter FIVE

I WAS A GOOD STUDENT despite the Raven's cruelty. I looked at it as a game and practiced harder at reading, writing, and arithmetic than any other girl in my class. Not only did I enjoy proving my teacher wrong, but I figured I had to learn as much as I could that year, because I planned to leave on the *North Star* with my parents the next summer and never return. While my schoolmates played cards and made dolls during their recreation time, I chose to read. I started with the simple readers we were given, tracing my finger

*See photo
on page 100.*

over the words again and again, trying to sound them out and decipher what they meant, but by spring I was reading books like the ones that Rosie had. I bided my time and waited to escape the Raven.

When the first boats began to appear, I could hardly believe the time had come. It would not be long before my parents arrived. However, on one of the boats was a letter from my father. The *North Star,* along with the other schooners, had not made it home to Banks Island the summer before. They had been stranded on a smaller island by an early freeze. The hunting and trapping had not been as successful there, and the entire group had decided to do their trading in Tuktoyaktuk instead of coming all the way to Aklavik, for fear of being caught by the ice again.

See photo on page 101.

I was devastated. This could not be happening. By now I could read and knew my times tables as well as Katherine, and I was ready to go home. It was

time—and my parents were not going to come for me. Not sure if they would ever come for me, I cried until the letter was so soaked with tears, it tore in my hands. That night I had a nightmare. I dreamed I was locked beneath the Raven's habit with many other children. She cackled and laughed as we tried to break free, straining against its weight, knowing that we would never see our parents again.

Outside, men competed in athletics and women gossiped, and everyone sang and danced and shared the stories of our ancestors, while I delivered meals to the sick patients in the hospital. It did not take me long to discover that being a nurse was not the glamorous job I had imagined. I would have given anything to be with my people eating dry meat and muktuk—delicious tiny cubes of whale blubber and skin.

If I could not go home, or even to the games, the least the nuns could do was continue to teach me. But of course, they did not.

While I was not the only child who did not go home that summer, I was lonely without Agnes. She was able to return home to her family, as they were now living in Tuktoyaktuk. But the nuns did their very best not to return any of us. Keeping us at the school was an easy way to ensure that we would return each fall, which was important to them. It wasn't just the chores—they were paid by the government per student, and plucking us from our homes and keeping us in their nests was a money-making business.

MY SUMMER SCHEDULE provided little time even for reading, and I was happy to have regular classes begin again in the fall. The Raven was nearly bearable in comparison with the long hours of chores and hospital work. But when the wind turned cold again in October, the whole of the North seemed to come down with a sickness called smallpox, and the hospital filled to capacity. Our classes were halted, once again, just weeks after they had resumed. Into November, as the hours of darkness lengthened day by day, we worked around the clock with the nuns and the men who were hired to do the chores that we children could not do. We were instructed to call these men Brothers, but they were far from being family. I was pretty sure that some did not even believe in God.

I was no stranger to hard work—life in the North required it—but I really disliked working in the hospital. The trappers were ill tempered and the sick women cried for their babies. Caring for them required so much of us that I longed for the return of the midnight sun to light the pages of my book, because I could only find a moment's peace to read very late in the evening. As it was, I held fairy tales and adventures to the window, desperate for escape, squinting in the darkness to catch the aquamarine glow of the northern lights.

Many of my classmates fell ill eventually, tiny blistering sores rising on their skin and covering them

See photo on page 101.

northern lights: curtains of light, often green or greenish-blue, seen near the magnetic North Pole, most visible at the equinoxes (March and September). Also known as aurora borealis.

with the same pox we had seen on the patients we attended. I no longer complained of the work. At least I did not have small-pox. As I watched several of the other children fall under the torment of the disease, I forgot both my exhaustion and my desire to read, and worked hard to do what was necessary.

I had been emptying bedpans and basins of dirty cleaning water for many hours one day when my bladder started to hurt. I needed to hurry, but each time I made for the door, the Raven gave me another job to do. I pressed my bare knees together and shuffled from bed to bed, trying to ease the feverish patients. If only the pain would disappear, or the Raven would go away. My bladder grew heavier and heavier. I crossed my legs and tried not to think about it.

Just when I thought my whole tummy would burst, I noticed that the Raven was busy chastising Katherine. I would have laughed out loud, if it had not meant I would pee myself. This was my chance, and I ran through the door. The hallway was like the tundra—it went on forever. No matter how far I traveled, I never seemed to get anywhere.

See photo on page 102.

I was just one step from the doorway—when from out of nowhere appeared two hungry eyes, like those of an owl. They leveled themselves to the height of my nose. The mouth beneath them opened, baring fishy, yellow teeth, and instead of letting out an owly *whoooo*, the mouth growled. I felt something warm run down my legs, as the Brother ran off laughing.

Before I could make it back to my room to clean myself up, the coarse voice of the Raven called after me. Her heels clicked and scraped against the floor, as she came closer. There was no escape.

"You are a filthy child," she said, when she saw what I had done.

I told her about the Brother, but she accused me of lying. To educate me, she left me shivering on the front

58

lawn with a bucket of hot soapy water. I didn't need to look up to know that the other girls would be looking through the window and laughing, while I washed out my canvas bloomers.

AS PEOPLE BECAME WELL again in late November, classes resumed. By then, I had read *Alice's Adventures in Wonderland* four times. Rosie had been telling the truth: Alice had not been hunting the rabbit at all. I would have brought its pelt back for my father.

One day, the Raven entered the classroom and told us that we would write letters home to our parents. I could hardly restrain myself in my seat. Not only did I long to make my father proud by telling him all that I had learned, and about all of the books I had read, but I wanted to ask him to come for me the next time the sun returned to melt the ice. We dipped our pens in our ink wells and wrote *Dear Mother and Father,* as instructed. For most of the students, the exercise was almost pointless. Many of their parents were unable to read English, just as my mother could not. Next we were told to write *I love it here at the school. The nuns have been very kind to us.*

Kind? That was a stretch. Instead, I wrote:

Dear Mother and Father,

I hate this school. You were right. The food is awful and the nuns are very mean. They won't even let me wear the stockings you bought for me. As you can see, I have already learned to read and write. Please, come to get me as soon as you can. I am ready to go home.

Love,
Olemaun

I did not hear the rest of what the Raven dictated, but it didn't matter. I had written everything that I needed to say. I passed my letter to the front with the others.

Now, all I had to do was wait—or so I thought. Two days later, the Raven called me to her desk. "This is not what you were told to write," she said, tearing my letter in half and throwing it in the trash can. "Now, write it again, so it reads like this." She handed me a slip of paper to copy from.

The other children were dismissed to go and play in the recreation room, but I was held back to write my letter. I stared at the ceiling and imagined I was bundled in hides, safe in my father's dogsled, whizzing through a snowy valley of white. I counted the stars and watched the northern lights dance, frost clinging to my nostrils.

Sister MacQuillan glimpsed me through the door as she floated by. She stopped, stepped into the room, and looked over my shoulder.

"It's all right, Margaret," she said. "You may go to dinner now."

The Raven scowled at me when I handed in my letter. All I had written was, *Dear Mother and Father.* She would have held me there all night, had it not been for Sister MacQuillan, but it would not have mattered. Nothing could make me write that I loved the school.

I found a seat next to Agnes in the refectory. "What's wrong?" she asked.

"The Raven won't let me send a letter to my parents asking them to come and get me."

"Don't worry. I overheard two nuns talking today. Next week we are going over to CHAK to broadcast a message to our parents. You can tell them then."

CHAK was a new radio station that had been established in the North not long before I started school. My parents loved it. They would be listening.

The following week, we were marched over to the small wooden building in the middle of town and lined up outside in the dark. My knees nearly froze solid in the frigid winter air. Christmas was less than three weeks away. The nuns were crazy to make us children stand outside.

I had practiced and practiced what I intended to say, but when I stepped inside the warm building I was handed a piece of paper with writing on it. *Hello, Mom! Hello, Dad!* it read. *Merry Christmas! I miss you, but the nuns here treat us like family and school is very fun.*

See photo on page 102.

I did not know what the nuns thought they were going to accomplish with these messages home. The

false praise of the school would be lost on the many non-English-speaking parents.

"And if you do not say what you are told to, we will cut the transmission," the Raven informed me. "Is that clear?"

I should have known. Why would this message be any different?

I stood in front of the microphone. *Mother, Father, get me out of here, please. Take me home! I'm freezing and my teacher is wicked and mean*, I thought, but I said nothing. Not one word. I never stopped talking at home; my silence would surely tell them that something was wrong.

Chapter SIX

EVERY TIME A BLACKBOARD was to be cleaned or a floor mopped, the Raven was sure to put me to work doing it. I prayed that she would forget about me altogether, but her attentions only grew with the daylight hours. I returned to the dormitory one Saturday night in April, after an evening of the Raven's education. She was not pleased with my silence at the radio station and cleaning the nasty chicken coop was how she made me pay for it.

My raw fingers stung as I opened the door to an

See photo on page 103.

explosion of excitement. Agnes was giddily twirling around her bed. She kicked up a leg to show me.

"New stockings," she chirped, as I pulled my own slouching pair back up over my knees. "Aren't they beautiful? I bet they belonged to a fancy Toronto lady. Everyone is getting new stockings!"

Maybe the outsiders had come to their senses: I might just survive another winter of the Raven's education if I could get my hands on some new stockings. I stripped off my old ones and threw them on the pile, praying for a nice black pair, like Agnes's. I closed my eyes and waited my turn.

The Raven swooped in. "I saved a special pair for you," she said.

I stared. I closed my eyes again and slowly opened them wider and wider. I looked to the other girls and examined their stockings, and then turned back to my own.

The Raven had played a heartless trick on me. Embarrassment and anger swelled in my heart. These stockings could never have belonged to a fancy lady from Toronto.

"They're . . . they're red!" I stammered.

The Raven cackled as I ran to my bed beneath the window. It was bad enough that I was much larger than the other girls, and that my calf muscles were far more pronounced than those of my skinny-legged classmates, but now I had to wear the only bright red stockings in the school. I pulled them on to see if they were really as bad as I thought. They were worse. The stockings made my legs look even bigger than they already were. I stared at my big fat red legs. I looked like a plump-legged circus clown.

The laughter of the other girls enveloped me. It wrapped a million fingers around me and would not let go. As soon as the Raven was gone, I pulled my favorite book from underneath my pillow and imagined the Raven in the role of the Queen of Hearts.

See photo on page 103.

THE NEXT MORNING, I crept into the refectory late, my calves on fire in those hideous stockings. A buzz filled the room and swarmed about the tables. I felt dizzy. Every eye was burning into my legs. I wanted to dissolve into my bowl of mush.

Katherine turned and pointed. "Fatty Legs," she laughed, bits of food spilling from her mouth.

"Fatty Face," I called back.

The Raven caught me by the ear. "If you cannot eat nicely with the other children, maybe you would be happier tending to the dirty laundry for the rest of the week," she said. "Now, get going. There's a fire waiting for you."

I could hardly will my feet to move under the weight of my big fat red legs, knowing that everyone was getting a good look at them as I sidled down the aisle and out the door of the dining hall.

My chest ached. As I stirred the dirty clothing, a tear escaped my eye. It fell from my chin onto the scalding cast iron vat.

Ptsch.

The tear bubbled and vanished with a poof of steam.

"Aha!" I whispered. In that moment, I knew how I would stop all of this Fatty Legs business.

I had only to await my chance.

FOR THE NEXT FEW DAYS, the other girls made sounds like the heavy beat of a drum when I walked by. *"Boom! Boom! Boom!"* they called.

They could go ahead and have their laugh at my expense. It would be short-lived. Although when they started calling Agnes "Skinny Legs," I felt like setting out across the ice and walking home, then and there. Katherine teased Agnes so mercilessly that one day, for the very first time, Agnes did not pick me first to be on her team at recreation time. My resolve hardened. I could not lose my best friend.

The time had come to put my plan into action. Each morning as I pulled up my red stockings, my spirit rose. All I needed was opportunity.

On Sunday, my last day in the laundry room, it came. I looked around to make sure I was alone. The Raven usually went to her room after church to listen to the radio, and the Brother who helped to stoke the fire had gone out for a cigarette. I stripped off the stockings, and in one quick motion, shoved them into the blazing fire beneath the vat. The hideous things sizzled and crackled in the fire as they shrank before my eyes and vaporized into a thin wisp of smoke.

I smiled with satisfaction. I would not be bested. The Raven was about to find out what I was made of, and was she ever in for a shock.

She flailed like a fish on the ice when she noticed my bare legs, and threw her hands up in the air. "How dare you enter the refectory without your stockings? You will be dressed appropriately at all times. Now, go back and put them on this instant."

"I can't," I told her.

"And why not?"

"I just can't."

She could scream all she wanted. It wouldn't bring them back.

She rose from the table. "Margaret, you go back to your room and get those stockings, right now."

"They aren't there."

"Margaret Pokiak." Her beady black eyes bore holes into me. "I will find those stockings. Rest assured."

The hatchlings weren't giggling anymore. Everyone had to help in the search. We tore the crowded dorm room apart and scoured the whole school from top to bottom. We emptied our trunks and the nuns rummaged through our belongings. The Raven had each girl strip her bedding and flip her mattress.

"You had better tell her where those stockings are," Katherine said to me.

"Nope," I said. "No one's going to call me Fatty Legs, ever again."

"You think you're pretty brave, don't you?" She leaned forward and fixed her eyes on me, but I wasn't scared of her. I stood my ground.

"You *are* brave, Margaret," said Sister MacQuillan,

stepping around the corner. Katherine moved away from me and rejoined the other Gwich'in girls. The Swan handed me a key. "Go and get your stockings from the storeroom."

Agnes met my eyes from where she stood over her upturned mattress and smiled.

It was time for lights out when I returned with the stockings. I would have to wait until the next morning to put them on.

When the morning came, I put on my beautiful thick pair of gray wool stockings. They were gorgeous. After our chores and prayers, I ran back up to the dormitory bursting with pride. I danced between the beds, whirling around for so long that I missed breakfast. I was eager to get to class on time, though. I sprang down the hallway stairs, like a gray-legged wolf.

The Raven choked on the claw she had been nibbling, as I strutted my sleek new legs past her desk. Her face turned as red as seal's blood on snow. Sister

MacQuillan stepped through the doorway and headed straight for the Raven. She whispered something in her ear, and the Raven blew up like a ptarmigan balloon. Her ears nearly popped off. Then Sister MacQuillan tilted her head gracefully in my direction. A faint smile crossed her lips. I knew the Raven would no longer be free to "educate" me as much as she had been.

The Raven thought she was there to teach me a few things, but in the end, I think it was she who learned a lesson: Be careful what birds you choose to pluck from their nests. A wren can be just as clever as a raven.

Chapter SEVEN

A T TIMES, I FELT as though my parents might forget me—forget that they had a daughter in a faraway school. And the dream returned often. The one in which I was trapped beneath the weight of the Raven's habit. I would never escape.

School ended, once again, and I soberly prepared for another summer of delivering meals to the sick and wishing I were back home. However, with the first boats came a new letter. It asked that I travel to Tuktoyaktuk on one of the school's boats. My family would meet me there. They wanted me to come home! The first time my father had written to me in English, it was to say he would not be coming for me. That letter had been painful to read. Now, at last, I could revel in each of the words he had penned on the page. I had not been forgotten. His letter proved it.

I couldn't wait to put the Raven at my back and some distance between us. The only outsider I would miss would be Sister MacQuillan. I could not leave without thanking her, so after I had packed my things, I went to her office.

"I am grateful for your kindness," I told her.

"You are a strong child. You will go far in life." She touched the top of my head and a tingle ran down to my toes. Then she pulled a book from her drawer and gave it to me. "I know how much you love this one."

It was my very own copy of *Alice's Adventures in Wonderland*. "Thank you," I said, taking the book and pressing it to my chest.

"You will be very missed, Margaret." She paused a

moment. Then she changed her words: "You will be very missed, Olemaun."

She had called me by my name—the name I had not heard in two years. Hearing it now brought tears to my eyes.

"Qugyuk," I said, pointing to her. It was the name I had always associated with her: Swan.

Sister MacQuillan elongated her neck and raised her arms like she would take flight. We both giggled.

I was sorry that I would not see the swan-like Sister again. I was sure that once I told my father about the Raven, he would never allow me to return to school.

See photo on page 104.

THE TRIP TO TUKTOYAKTUK aboard the Roman Catholic boat, the *Immaculata,* was crowded. We had no choice but to sit quietly as hour after hour drifted by and turned to day after day. The journey back to the ocean took much longer than the journey into the delta had because many children had to be dropped off on the way down the Peel and Mackenzie Rivers. Wherever the boat stopped, we children would scramble up the banks of the shore and run around wildly, stretching our legs and enjoying the space.

When we reached the mouth of the Mackenzie River, the saltwater smell of the bay unlocked distant memories and made me long for Banks Island. At that point, I was truly free of the outsiders' school. I had left it behind me, back past the tree line in a tangled cluster of waterways. After two long years, I was out on the open water, where I belonged. Each nightless day in that tiny boat had taken forever to pass. Now we were so close!

See photo on page 104.

We made our way across the bay to Tuktoyaktuk, and there was the *North Star,* anchored in the harbor. The moment was here at last. The *Immaculata* had only grazed the shore when I gave Agnes a quick hug and leaped from the boat. The Brothers couldn't stop me.

My father stood right there on the shore. He would have given them a what for if they had tried.

I was safe.

But my mother didn't know me.

"Not my girl," she told the Brothers. "Not *my* girl."

Those three words thudded between my ears, over and over, and I feared the Brothers would take me away with them again. I had not seen my mother in two years. She remembered a pale eight-year-old with pudgy cheeks. I was now tall, lean, very tanned, and ten years old.

My father knew me right away. He wrapped his arms around my body, and after a moment, so did my mother and siblings.

My mother had brought a small package of all of the things that I had liked to eat, assuming that I would be eager to try them once again. However, the food was strange and difficult to eat. It felt greasy and was salty, with a strong smell. I was not sure I would ever be able to eat it. My mother cried and said I was now an outsider. On the way to our camp, she asked my father to buy me some of their outsider-food from the Hudson's Bay store in Tuktoyaktuk. He laughed and told her that I was still Inuvialuit, and when I got hungry enough, I would eat. Eventually, I did.

*See photo
on page 105.*

Before bed that first night, I read to my family from the book that Sister MacQuillan had given me. When I was done, I crawled under the warm hides, gazed at the glow of the embers from my father's pipe, and drifted off to sleep.

My curiosity had led me far away, and now here I was, after two years, satisfied that I now knew what happened to girls who went down rabbit holes.

After THE STORY

THE YEAR FOLLOWING MY return home was one of the happiest of my life. The excitement of hunting with my father, the pleasures of fishing with my mother, and the fun of seeking out goose eggs with my siblings all held new wonder for me. I was certain that I would not go back to the school in Aklavik for anything.

However, my three younger sisters grew curious. After they pestered my father non-stop, and the government made school attendance a condition

See photo on page 105.

for receiving child benefits, he gave in and agreed that they, too, could go and learn to read. I tried to warn them, just as Rosie had tried to warn me. Their hair would be cut, I told them. They would have to do many chores and kneel on their knees to ask for forgiveness. It was no use.

We Inuvialuit are headstrong. Thankfully, we are also resilient. So, reluctantly, I went with them—to make sure that they did not forget that wrens can be just as clever as ravens and owls.

Afterword

INDIGENOUS CHILDREN LIKE Margaret-Olemaun
Pokiak were equipped with many skills that allowed
them to survive and thrive even in extreme envi-
ronments. They also had the benefit of the ancestral
knowledge of all the generations of grandparents before
them to know how to live comfortably where they were.
By the time Olemaun was 10, she could command her
own dogsled team and was very handy with a hunting rifle. When Europeans arrived in North America/
Turtle Island, they saw land they wanted to farm, log,
mine, and build cities on. However, taking over that

See photo on page 106.

land meant they would have to remove the people who already lived there and erase the inhabitants' traditional way of living on the land. One way of doing this was to send Indigenous children to residential schools, where those traditional skills were replaced by skills needed to do menial jobs for the outsiders who were taking over their territories. Indigenous languages were forbidden at the schools and replaced with English or French. This was done not only to prepare the children for the low skill jobs the outsiders had planned for them, but also to ensure they forgot their own languages. If an Indigenous person could no longer communicate in their Indigenous language, they could not receive vital knowledge from their grandparents, knowledge keepers, and elders back home, who were unlikely to communicate in English or French.

Some parents, despite knowing the horrific reputation of the schools, made the extremely difficult choice to send their children because they could see no other way to prepare them for a rapidly changing world. Most children, however, were forcibly taken, even kidnapped. The churches that ran the schools were paid a fee for each child attending, so they wanted to keep enrollment high. Just as Olemaun had to work at the school in Aklavik, Indigenous children throughout Canada and the U.S. were responsible for emptying honey buckets of bathroom waste, scrubbing floors and hauling firewood, and all the chores associated with running the schools. They were also made to do extra labor to bring profits to the schools, such as working in hospitals, running trap lines, building furniture, and working on ranches and farms, with some never actually seeing the inside of a classroom. Children were exposed to diseases such as tuberculosis in crowded unsanitary schools where they worked long hours, were fed poorly, and were disciplined harshly. Many of the teachers and administrators at these schools were unqualified to educate the children in their care, and some were placed there by the church as a means of punishment for crimes against children in their own communities.

At the school in Aklavik, Olemaun's clothing was taken away, her hair was cut, and she was not allowed to speak her language. The schools were meant to strip Indigenous children of their culture and skills. Being

See photo
on page 106.

told that a European style dress was more appropriate to wear in the High Arctic than a caribou-lined parka had long-lasting psychological effects on the children, who were taught to question both the practical knowledge of their people and their own common sense. In addition, children returning home were often considered outsiders themselves. No longer able to communicate with even their own parents, they were shunned for the new ways they had been forced to adopt. For example, Indigenous children were expected to be responsible, to take initiative, and to act when they saw a job that needed to be done. In a traditional setting, they were capable and acted with confidence. But at the schools, children could expect abuse for speaking or daring to move without first receiving permission. When they returned home, they would see a job that needed to be done, but they would wait to be asked to do it. It was then assumed they were lazy, when really, they were scared. The children who attended residential schools were not raised by parents. They were raised in hostile institutions, without hugs, kisses, or bedtime stories, in a world where there were no babies or children under the age of four. When they grew up, they had no healthy examples to draw on to show them how to parent. They didn't grow up seeing how a mother feeds a baby or potty trains a toddler. The challenge of becoming a parent themselves was enormous. Add to this that schools were known to marry off some of the girls as soon as they graduated, commonly around the age of fourteen. The wounds of the abuse they endured run so deep they will be felt for several generations. They pass from parent to child to grandchild, and each does what they can to heal.

We owe a massive debt to all the elders and knowledge keepers who carry on their traditional ways, speak their traditional languages, have the courage to bring their love to the world, and are brave enough to share the stories of how they endured the horrors of the Indian Residential/Boarding School systems in Canada and the U.S. From the time they were children, they have been facing down oppression by nations that have systemically sought to kill their culture and silence their voices.

Today, the healing continues as many survivors and

their children work to shed the shame imposed on them from colonization. We now have our first generation of parents untouched directly by residential school, and with that we are seeing a renaissance of cultural pride and reclamation. Youth proudly introduce themselves with their traditional names and the communities they belong to. Grandparents volunteer countless hours to revive languages for their grandchildren's generation, after years of believing it wasn't safe to teach those languages to their children. Participation in traditional ceremonies is sharply on the rise. Traditional communities continue to reclaim and to heal, and lost generations continue to find their ways home or to build strong urban communities, with healing circles, drumming, hand games, athletic games, powwows, storytelling, songs, handicrafts, ceremonies, and innovative and creative contemporary ways to express Indigenous cultural realities—such as books like this one.

Christy Jordan-Fenton

Acknowledgments

THE AUTHOR WISHES TO thank everyone who helped along the journey, including Robert N. Stephenson, Kate Messner, Judith Diehl, Stella Lisa Samuels, Maggie DeVries, Pam Robertson, and Laura Edlund, and everyone at Annick Press. Also Debbie Reese.

Olemaun's SCRAPBOOK

Me and my family on the
five day journey to Aklavik.
I'm second from the right.

*My older half-sister, Ayouniq, had been
plucked before I was born, but we called
her "Rosie" after her return.*

In this photo, Rosie wears Inuvialuit-
style kamiks on her feet.

Rosie turned, pulled apart the flaps of the tent door, and disappeared through the tunnel in the snow that formed the entrance to our home.

We traveled by dogsled for several hours, until we came to a place where game was plentiful.

Me and my father/*aapang* sitting on top of the schooner, the *North Star*.

My mother/*amaamang*.

94

We traveled with six other schooners, each carrying as many as six or seven families. Our schooner was the North Star.

Beyond Tuktoyaktuk, the pingos rose out of the ocean like goose eggs with smashed-in tops.

Pingos are formed when a large lump of ice pushes soil up to make a temporary mountain.

95

*We came to Reindeer Station, a settlement of herders,
and excitement consumed me.*

*We made our way down the plank and scrambled up the steep muddy
slope to the settlement our own great-grandfather, Old Man Pokiak, had
founded as a trading post.*

My great-grandfather poses with his family in Aklavik, 1922.
When I went to school, the houses in Aklavik were similar to this one.

A tractor drives past the Hudson's
Bay Company store in Aklavik.

*Behind them stood two immense wooden buildings, so much larger than our
schooner, with rows and rows of windows. I had forgotten how big these buildings were.*

This photo, taken from the water, shows the school on the left and the hospital on
the right. In the school building, the boys' dormitory is on the left wing, while the
girls' dormitory is on the right. The classrooms were on the bottom floor.

An enormous photograph hung on one of the clean, painted walls. In it, an outsider wore a fancy sash. Medallions like large coins hung from his chest—I would learn later that he was king of all of the outsiders. They told me he was also my king.

This king is George VI, who ruled from 1936 to 1952.

Letters, like those from Rosie's books, decorated the walls of the classroom. I stared at them, trying to decipher what they might mean.

This photo shows a classroom in the school that I went to.

98

The nuns starched the peaks they wore and sometimes we could see the place where they shaved their heads underneath.

An Anglican school room in Hay River, in the Northwest Territories, similar to the one I sat in.

Going on outings like berry picking was supposed to be fun.
But the island I came from had no trees, so the bushes scared me.

My sisters and cousins playing
in the space between the school
and the hospital.

When the first boats began to appear, I could hardly believe the time had come. It would not be long before my parents arrived.

In this photo, the community waits on the banks for the mail boats to arrive.

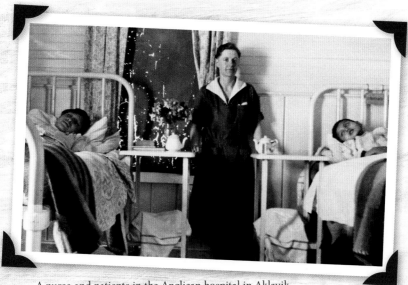

A nurse and patients in the Anglican hospital in Aklavik. This hospital was similar to the one where I worked.

The Brothers at my school dressed like this.

The radio station where I refused to speak looked like this.

Unloading a barge of firewood in the spring.
I'm in the middle.

As soon as the Raven was
gone, I pulled my favorite book
from underneath my pillow and
imagined the Raven in the role
of the Queen of Hearts.

Alice meets the Queen of Hearts.

The trip to Tuktoyaktuk aboard the Roman
Catholic boat, the Immaculata, *was crowded.*

We made our way across the bay to Tuktoyaktuk, and
there was the North Star, anchored in the harbor.

My brother Ernest, my father and mother,
and my little sister Millie, in front.

Here is a typical winter scene in Aklavik when I was a child.

Many Indigenous children like me from across Canada and the U.S. were sent to church-run schools. This is a picture of the girls at the Anglican residential school in Aklavik, taken about the time I was at the Catholic residential school.

Me when I was about 16. I made this outfit myself. You can see how much I love sewing and doing beading and embroidery.

Photo CREDITS

xviii: (Olemaun and her sisters) courtesy of Margaret-Olemaun Pokiak-Fenton

2 and 116: basic map outlines by Map Resources; additions by Lisa Hemingway

92: (top, Pokiak family) Holman Photohist. and Oral History Research Cttee/NWT Archives/ N-1990-004: 0068; (bottom, Rose Pokiak) M. Meikle, Library and Archives Canada/PA-101772

93: (top, snow tent) R. Knights/NWT Archives/N-1993-002-0158; (bottom, dogsled) Frank and Frances Carpenter collection, LC-USZ62-34903. Courtesy of Library of Congress Prints and Photographs Division

94: (top and bottom, Margaret-Olemaun's father and mother) courtesy of Margaret-Olemaun Pokiak-Fenton

95: (top, *North Star* schooner) Wilkinson/NWT Archives/N-1979-051-1178; (bottom, pingo) Hunt/ NWT Archives/N-1979-062: 0008

96: (top, Reindeer Station) Canada. Affaires indiennes et du Nord/Library and Archives Canada/ PA-203204; (bottom, Old Man Pokiak) Jackson/NWT Archives/N-1979-004-0261

97: (top, Hudson's Bay store in Aklavik) K. Lang/NWT Archives/N-1979-007-0027; (bottom, school and hospital) Fleming/NWT Archives/N-1979-050: 0042

98: (top, George VI) G. Eric and Edith Matson Photograph Collection, LC-DIG-matpc-14736. Courtesy of Library of Congress Prints and Photographs Division; (bottom, classroom interior) ECE/NWT Archives/G-1999-088:0142

99: (top, two nuns) Saich/NWT Archives/N-1990-003:0042; (bottom, school in Hay River) YK Museum Soc./NWT Archives/N-1979-056-0057

100: (top, students on barge) Wilkinson/NWT Archives/N-1979-051-1191; (bottom, Margaret-Olemaun's sisters and cousin) courtesy of Margaret-Olemaun Pokiak-Fenton

101: (top, waiting for the mail boat) J.L. Robinson/Library and Archives Canada/PA-102235; (bottom, hospital) Fleming/NWT Archives/N-1979-050-0053

102: (top, brothers and boys) Sacred Heart Parish/NWT Archives/N-1992-255-0401; (bottom, radio station) Wilkinson/NWT Archives/N-1979-051-0465S

103: (top, hauling firewood) courtesy of Margaret-Olemaun Pokiak-Fenton; (bottom, Alice and the Queen of Hearts) illustration by Sir John Tenniel, scan © istockphoto.com/Darren Hendley

104: (top, the *Immaculata*) Library and Archives Canada/PA- 101292; (bottom, Tuktoyaktuk) Dept. of the Interior/NWT Archives/G-1989-006:0082

105: (top, Margaret-Olemaun's parents, sister, and brother) courtesy of Margaret-Olemaun Pokiak-Fenton; (bottom, dogsled in Aklavik) Gar Lunney/National Film Board of Canada. Photothèque/Library and Archives Canada/PA-163040

106: (top, schoolgirls) Fleming/NWT Archives/N-1979-050-0954; (bottom, Margaret-Olemaun at 16) courtesy of Margaret-Olemaun Pokiak-Fenton

114: (Olemaun with her mother and her sisters Mabel and Bessie) courtesy of Margaret-Olemaun Pokiak-Fenton.

137: (Christy Jordan-Fenton) courtesy of Micky Wiswedel; (Margaret-Olemaun Pokiak-Fenton) courtesy of Allison Peck

Special thanks to the staff at NWT Archives, Library and Archives Canada, and the Brechin Group.

A Note on Language

We have updated select terms throughout *Fatty Legs* to reflect the developments and evolutions in language that have emerged since the book was first published ten years ago.

We have used *Inuvialuit* more often in this edition to correctly distinguish from the broader term *Inuit*. We have also been more specific with the use of *Indigenous Peoples* versus *Indigenous people*: *Peoples* is used to indicate the collective, referring to multiple groups or tribal nations, while *people* refers to the individuals within the different collectives. We have also substituted *Native* with *Indigenous* to follow current best practices as set out in *Elements of Indigenous Style* by Gregory Younging (Brush Education, 2018). Perhaps most importantly, we have updated the treatment of Margaret-Olemaun's own name. Since the initial publication of *Fatty Legs*, she has reclaimed the name Olemaun. While the original text referred to her most often as *Margaret*, this edition more frequently uses *Margaret-Olemaun* whenever it mentions the present day. *Olemaun* is used to reference the author when she was a girl, as well as in reference to her inner-most self; *Margaret* is mostly used when depicting the author's time in residential school. Despite our adherence to certain guidelines within this text, it is proper to use the specific term or name pre-ferred by each Indigenous person. In all cases of language choice, but especially with names and tribal affiliations, self-determination for Indigenous people should be the guiding principle.

A Note on the Writing Process

PROBABLY THE MOST FREQUENTLY asked question we have received jointly since *Fatty Legs* was released in 2010 is: What is your process for working together? Maybe you are blessed with an elder in your life who has other worlds hidden inside of them. And maybe like me, you find yourself pulled into those other places and times with each story that elder shares. That is how it is between Margaret-Olemaun and me. When she tells me a story, she takes me there with her. Later, I sit replaying those moments she has shared with me, over and over in my head, until I see how each moment fits together. I ask Margaret-Olemaun question after question to fill in the gaps of my understanding, and she patiently answers. I do research to learn more. I go back again and ask questions. Then one day the magic moment happens, like when the first day of summer would arrive on Margaret-Olemaun's arctic home of Banks Island, when the ice would break from the ocean, and she knew it was time to set sail. That's when I begin writing her stories into a narrative. Once I am done, I take it to Margaret-Olemaun. She tells me what I have misunderstood, what is a story only meant for me and not the public, and what she'd like to share in more depth. Then I go back and do another draft. Once she approves, and feels I have captured her voice and her experiences accurately, I send the manuscript to an editor (Maggie DeVries for *Fatty Legs* and *A Stranger at Home*). The editor is like the navigator, pointing out both obstacles and better routes to take along the journey back to Olemaun's childhood. I use the input to revise the story, asking Margaret-Olemaun even more questions and doing more research. Once Margaret-Olemaun feels the manuscript has arrived where she wants readers to visit, it goes back to the editor for further navigational fine-tuning. We repeat this process until Margaret-Olemaun's stories have emerged into a written form that can transport readers to the precise place and time she has shown me through her oral stories. The stories of elders are like time machines; we hope you are moved by your journey through this one to meet Margaret-Olemaun.

Christy Jordan-Fenton

Read on for the first chapter of the acclaimed follow-up
to *Fatty Legs*, also available from Annick Press

a stranger at home

A True Story

Christy JORDAN-FENTON *&*
Margaret-Olemaun POKIAK-FENTON

Artwork by Liz Amini-Holmes

Me with my sisters Mabel and Bessie and our mother,
sitting in front of the smokehouse.

Introduction

MY NAME IS OLEMAUN Pokiak—that's OO-*lee-mawn*. Such a name probably sounds strange to you. I can understand, because there was a time in my life when it sounded strange to me, too. Would you believe that at one point I could scarcely remember my own name or even speak the same language as my mother? Well, it's true. The outsiders had locked my tongue with the spell of their "education." But I was named for a stone that sharpens a knife, and I was strong. I could not be worn down.

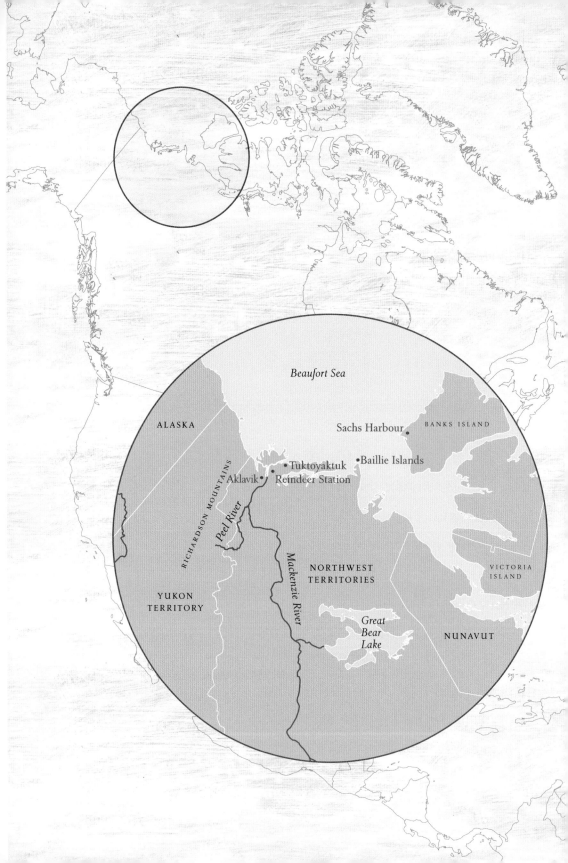

Beaufort Sea

ALASKA

BANKS ISLAND

Sachs Harbour

Baillie Islands

Tuktoyaktuk

Aklavik   Reindeer Station

RICHARDSON MOUNTAINS

Peel River

Mackenzie River

NORTHWEST
TERRITORIES

VICTORIA
ISLAND

YUKON
TERRITORY

Great
Bear
Lake

NUNAVUT

Chapter ONE

THE BOAT CRUNCHED TO a stop against the shore. My fingers gripped into the side of it as I propelled my body over the edge. "No," I heard my friend Agnes call with a restrained cry. The shore was packed with people, though Tuktoyaktuk was very small. I pushed through the crowd, my canvas shoes rolling on the tiny pebbles as I searched for my family. It had been so long since I had seen them.

I HEARD A VOICE I recognized—it was my mother's. She was speaking to my siblings. I turned and followed it, making my way through the throng to where she stood, with my two-year-old brother Ernest tied to her back and my sisters Mabel and Elizabeth still looking up at the boat for me to disembark. I wondered why my father had not run to meet me the minute my feet hit the shore, but he was not with them. I stood proudly before my mother and siblings and waited for them to rush toward me.

My mother gave me a strange look, as if to question why I was standing before her. I smiled, but she crossed her arms and shook her head. "Not my girl. Not *my* girl," she shouted up to the dark-cloaked Brothers in the only English I had ever heard her speak.

I turned around to look at them where they stood, perched like birds of prey at the rail of the *Immaculata*. Their beady eyes studied me. If my mother didn't recognize me, I was certain that at any moment they would pounce on me and carry me back to their outsiders' nest up the Mackenzie Delta.

I could not understand how this could be happening. After days of being cramped aboard the small Roman Catholic boat, going ashore to stretch our legs only when we stopped to drop my classmates at their various Arctic settlements, this could not be my welcome. I had seen many mothers cry, and several fathers turn their heads to hide their own tears, as they welcomed back their children. After being gone for two years myself, I had all but lost hope that this day would come for me. But as each child left the boat on our way farther and farther north, my optimism grew. It grew until we reached the mouth of the Mackenzie River and then the hope inside of me erupted. The boat could barely contain the overwhelming anticipation I shared with my classmates. We had all waited for so long to be reunited with our parents in Tuktoyaktuk. Only my friend Agnes did not seem to be excited.

When the shore came into view, its long, thin peninsula stretching out to meet us, I felt so happy I was sure I could walk on water like Jesus had in the nuns' stories. Not even Agnes's reluctance or the Brothers' glares were enough to suppress the loud cheers that rose from the rest of us. The banks swelled with people, perhaps double the hundred or so who lived in Tuk most of the time. Like mine, other families had come from afar to collect their children. The trapper's daughter saw her father in the crowd and hugged her older brother, crying for joy. They had been gone just as long as I had been—two years. A short summer the year before had left many of us locked in by the ocean ice, with our parents unable to make it all the way to Aklavik to pick us up, or to arrange to get us from Tuk. The two older Gwich'in girls jumped up and down and waved to their family on the shore. The one named Katherine, who had always tried to bully me at school, was the happiest, because she was now thirteen and the outsiders could never make her go back to their school.

I wasn't going back either. I was going to tell my parents how awful the school was, so they would never make me leave the safety of our home on Banks Island ever again.

Now, on the shore, I looked from my unwelcoming mother up to where Agnes still stood on the deck of

Gwich'in: A tribe of the Dene Nation who live in the far northwestern part of Canada. The Gwich'in and the Inuvialuit have been known to feud with each other over resources.

the boat. She offered me a look of sympathy. Her own return had been painful the year before when she had gone home to Tuk for summer break.

I turned again to my mother. Our eyes were level; I was no longer the little girl who had always looked up at her. I was desperate to find a glint of recognition. There was none. Her face was still scrunched in protest, disbelieving that I was her child.

"Not my girl. Not my girl," she called again to the Brothers. I looked again to the boat behind me where they stood, and I tensed, ready to run if they made a move to come down and haul me away from my family. I was going to bolt. I'd run to the end of the peninsula and jump in the ocean if I had to. I was not returning to the school with them. I was never going to let them take me back.

It was their fault that my mother did not know me. It was because of the Brothers, the priests, and the nuns that she could no longer see who I was. They had cast an outsiders' spell on me with their endless chores and poor meals; they had turned me from the plump, round-faced girl my mother knew into a skinny, gaunt creature. And they had cut my long black hair into a short, choppy bob. They had spent two years making all these changes. I was now ten, and several inches taller than I had been when my parents left me at that school up the river in Aklavik.

I scanned the crowd for my father. He had to come and save me! One of the Brothers stepped onto the gangplank, and I leaned forward to run, but I was saved. My father emerged from the crowd and caught me in a tight embrace, the smoky smell of his parka wrapping around me. His strong hunter's hands stroked my hair.

"Olemaun," he said to me, the special name I had not heard for two years.

I whispered it to myself, "Oo-lee-maun."

The Inuit name my grandfather had given me felt strange to my tongue. I could not remember the last time I had thought of the name, let alone heard it spoken lovingly in my ear. I no longer felt worthy of it. It was like a beautiful dress that was far too big for me to wear. At the school I was known only as Margaret. Margaret was like a tight, scratchy dress, too small, like my school uniform. Not wanting my father to see that

Inuit: a general term for the Indigenous peoples who inhabit the Arctic regions of Canada, Greenland, Russia, and the United States. The term "Inuit" has largely replaced "Eskimo."

I was no longer his Olemaun, I buried my head against his chest.

I felt a soft touch, lighter than my father's, on my back. A familiar warm touch that worked its way into my heart with a tenderness I had not known for a long, long time. Only one person had ever touched me so sweetly—my mother. She slid her hand from my back and around my chest, reaching for my buried face. Her fingers were smooth against my chin. I shrank from them, filled with shame at having all but forgotten how affectionate a touch could be, and cried until my tears turned my father's parka wet.

My eight-year-old sister Elizabeth approached us first, while seven-year-old Mabel hung back. Then they joined us in a crushing hug, squeezing me in their embrace. Ernest reached out and touched my hair. All of those raven-eyed Brothers together could not have pried me from my family. I was safe. By the time we separated, they were pushing the *Immaculata* off the shore. They were moving on.

Katherine and the other Gwich'in girl would soon be leaving too. The supply barge had been in Aklavik when we left and it would arrive here in Tuk any day. After that, Katherine would go with her people, far to the southwest of Tuk, and I would never have to see her again.

The trapper's daughter and her brother would also be going. As I watched their mother kiss them, I wondered how they felt about the school. Being outsiders like the nuns and the priests, they had not found the school so hard, but I could tell by the way they clung to their mother that they had missed her, just as I had missed my own family. I caught Agnes's eye and she smiled at me, waving good-bye as she supported her mother as they walked up the bank and toward the tiny village of log cabins and tent homes. I hoped I would get another chance to see her before the barge arrived and I left with my family for our distant island.

My mother assumed I would be hungry after my long journey down the Delta, so she had brought along a package of all my favorite things. I couldn't wait to eat my mother's food, but when we settled on the beach and she unwrapped the package, I nearly lost my stomach. I was sickened by the pungent smell of whale blubber—muktuk, I remembered—the salty smell of dried fish, and the musky, gamey smell of meat and whipped caribou fat, which the outsiders called Eskimo ice cream, but it was nothing at all like ice cream. I crinkled my nose shut. The food smelled even worse than the swampy cabbage and disgusting bland, mushy porridge and beans we had to eat at the school.

My mother scrunched her brow and frowned. I could see how hurt she was that I was not eager to eat the food she had prepared for me.

At school we had been taught to pray before we ate, so I knew that God wanted me to drop to my knees to give thanks for the food I was about to receive, even though I was not so thankful for it. My family's eyes were on me, though, and I could not find the courage to pray in front of all of them. I made a note to give thanks later when I was alone and took a cubed chunk of blubber, muktuk, between my fingers. It felt like the bottom of my canvas runners.

Reluctantly, I put it in my mouth. It was rubbery and strange to chew and the taste made a gag come into my throat. I swallowed it down. The fish, which I reminded

126   *Muktuk is made from the blubber and skin of a whale.*
       It is enjoyed by the Inuit as a rich source of vitamin C.

myself was called pipsi, was salty and the Eskimo ice cream was so rich that I wanted to stick my head in the bay to wash away the taste. It all sat in my guts, filling me with a heavy, greasy feeling. I was hungry and I wanted to please my mother, but it was too much.

It was all too much: the way my little brother studied me as if I were a strange species of fish that had washed ashore, and the way my mother touched the ends of my hair and sobbed that her little girl had been turned into an outsider. I no longer belonged to my own family.

I assured my mother that I wasn't an outsider—that I was still her daughter—"No, no . . . It's me, I'm still the same"—but my words came out in English, which she could not understand, instead of Inuvialuktun, our native tongue. She cried even harder.

This was not the reunion I had dreamed of for two years, every long Arctic summer day without darkness and every longer sunless winter night. I just wanted to go home. I wanted us to load up the *North Star* right that minute and travel back across the Arctic Ocean to Banks Island, where my family always spent most of the year. Everything would be fine once we returned home, where I would be surrounded only by our small community of friends, far from all the outsiders, except for those who traveled with us and practiced our ways and not the ways of the nuns. Banks Island was a million miles from the school in Aklavik, far enough that the outsiders would be unlikely to come for me again. I needed the open ground beneath my feet. I needed to look out across the land, dotted only by our tents. I needed to climb the hill above the cemetery and see a world that was truly our own. In that world, the outsiders' spell on me could be broken, and I could forget.

"When do we leave for Banks Island?" I asked my

father, as I scanned the boats down the shore for my beloved *North Star*.

"Oh, Olemaun," he said to me in English, which he had learned at an outsiders' school many years ago, "we won't be going back. We have decided to stay here. We are going to try hunting and trading here in Tuk, and I can pick up extra work as a special constable for the RCMP. Mr. Carpenter will be leaving on the *North Star* without us."

I felt like a fish pulled up and flopped onto the ice— helpless and unable to find my way back to where I could breathe.

Instead of walking down the shoreline to our people's camp, next to the place where they had moored their schooners, we headed to the village. Over and over, I looked back at the bay. I was glad to be free of the Brothers, but I had not left the outsiders' world. I still was not home, and now I knew that I would not even be going there.

When we passed the Hudson's Bay Company store, my mother asked my father to stop and buy me some

RCMP: Royal Canadian Mounted Police. Canada's national police force.

schooner: a type of sailing vessel with masts.

129

of the outsiders' food. He laughed for a good while and told her that I was still Inuvialuit: when I got hungry enough, I would eat. My mother and I looked at each other. Neither of us was sure.

My spirits lifted when we made it to our canvas tent, which was set up on a wooden frame near a small lake a short way past the village. My father's dogs greeted me with yelps and barks. We had no animals at the school and I had missed them so much. I reached out to pet one of the nine sled dogs, but it nearly took my hand off.

"Wait until you wear our scent again," my father said, drawing back the canvas door.

I followed him into the darkness, and stood blinking as my eyes adjusted. Then I smiled a slow smile. It was exactly as I remembered it, just as it had been on Banks Island. The cookstove stood near the center, the table close to it, and my mother and father's bed was against the south wall. I leaned forward, ready to race for the spot under their bed where I had always slept, but stopped myself. It probably belonged to one of my siblings now. I looked to my mother and she

Hudson's Bay Company: the oldest surviving company in North America, incorporated by a royal charter in 1670. Hunters and trappers traded their pelts there for goods and supplies.

nodded with a smile. It was still mine! I dove under the big bed and onto the quilt that covered my small mattress. As I rolled to face the far side, I saw a small stack of my half-sister Rosie's books, which she must have left behind after her last visit. I was so excited to have something to read, but I was sorry I had missed seeing her. I wanted to tell her how bad I felt for not believing her when she warned me how awful the school was.

So many things had happened already and it was barely past lunch. I really needed to talk to someone like my big sister, who understood what I was going through, but I would have to settle for her books. I just wanted to curl up in my bed with them and drift off to sleep while the warm red glow of my father's pipe illuminated the dark tent.

My father peeked his head under the bed to see what I thought of the books. I hugged one to my chest. It was such a gift. My father had a kettle in his hand, and as he rose to put it on the stove I crawled out from my sleeping place, still hugging the book. My mother was at the foot of their bed, searching through the large wooden chest that held her things. At last, she pulled out one of her old parkas, a rich burgundy one embroidered with cream flowers. A detailed Delta braid ran around the hem. Lace decorated the shoulders and the wrists, and a stunning burst of wolf fur stood up around the hood. I remembered how beautiful she had looked in it long ago when we had come to a wedding here in Tuk. It was my favorite of her parkas. She looked at it a moment, then set it in my lap.

"For me?" I asked, pressing the fur to my face.

She smiled and nodded, understanding my gesture if not my words.

My sisters came through the door of the tent with my brother just as I pulled it over my head. I was now as big as my mother, and I felt very grown-up in her parka as I strutted around the tent for all my family to see. Elizabeth narrowed her eyes. I could tell she was envious, but I felt no pity. My mother's parka could not take away two years of shivering in my thin, ill-fitting uniform and canvas bloomers, nor could it make me forget the shame of being forced by a cruel nun to wear the school's only pair of bright red stockings. Being teased about how fat my legs looked in them had been the most

Delta braid, made by cutting pieces from long strips of fabric and layering them in a pattern, was used to decorate Mother Hubbard parkas.

humiliating experience of my life. But the fur of the parka's hood against my face helped me to feel like I was no longer that powerless girl. I needed my mother's parka in a way my sisters could never understand.

We drank tea and I did my best to answer my family's questions, my father translating everything at first. After a short time, a few of our words came back to me, but I was not able to respond to many of the questions on my own. It was frustrating. After only two years away, I could barely speak my own language. I had tried to preserve my memory of it, but what I had retained was like a clump of dry dirt that turned to dust in my hand. I wanted to laugh and giggle with my sisters, to tell them stories and teach them what I had learned, but my words were too few. I could speak to them only with a phrase or two and my heartfelt smiles.

"Mamaqtuq," I said, pointing to my tea—tastes good.

Everyone smiled, and my mother's smile was widest of them all.

My sisters pulled out two dolls that my father had made for them and begged me to play. I shook my head, because I had no doll of my own. At the school I had made a doll from scraps of fabric one of the sisters had given to me, but before I left I gave it to a smaller girl who was not going home.

My sisters pawed at me for attention. I had no words to tell them why I did not want to play their game. Mabel picked up a caribou-hide ball, and Elizabeth pulled me outside by the arm. We tossed the ball and ran until I forgot how homesick I was for Banks Island and how much I missed my friends from the school. It was so good to be back with my family.

By suppertime, I was very hungry, but still I could not eat. My mother stared at the table and cried. She worried that I would starve to death, but my father said something to her, then turned to me and spoke in English. "You'll eat when you're ready, won't you?" I was as unsure as my mother. The pain in my stomach was growing, and I wondered when my body would know that it was ready.

Before bed that first night, the family gathered around me as I read aloud from a book that a kind nun had given to me. Mabel was the same age I had been when I fell in love with the stories my big sister Rosie would read to me. Elizabeth was the same age I had been when my love for those stories and my desire to read them led me to the outsiders' school. I wished Rosie were there to watch our siblings listening as intently as I once had, even though they could not understand the words. My sisters' eyes grew wide in the dim light as they strained to comprehend what I was telling them. My brother Ernest sat on my lap and looked at the pictures. My father translated for me, and they all marveled that I could now decipher the outsiders' words. Even my mother was impressed.

I could tell by the way she kept looking up from her sewing.

Just as I was getting to a good part, my father looked up from his seat at the table and told us it was time to go to sleep. My mother tucked my sisters into the bed they shared and my brother got under the covers of my mother and father's bed. I crawled under the warm blankets beneath where my parents slept and gazed out at the glow of embers from my father's pipe. A heavy, ocean-like sleep settled over me and I drifted off to the dream time.

It wasn't Banks Island, but it *was* home. Even though I missed my friends at the school, nothing would ever make me go back. I belonged here in this tent with my family. I wasn't able to hide away on a distant island, but maybe, just maybe, the dark walls would ward off the outsiders' spell.

CHRISTY JORDAN-FENTON has been an infantry soldier, a bareback bronc rider, a survival instructor, and a wild pig farmer, among other things, and has lived in Australia, South Africa, and Vermont. She has a master's diploma in Human Rights and Forced Displacement from UPEACE, and is a Vital Voices Lead Fellow. She lives in Fort St. John, BC, but keeps an active traveling schedule. She and her mother-in-law, Margaret-Olemaun Pokiak-Fenton, speak with 100 audiences a year, from Anchorage to Havana. Her greatest passions are spending time with her three children, writing, and studying dance. In addition to being the grandmother of her children and the source of the childhood stories behind the four books they've created together, Margaret is also Jordan-Fenton's best friend and partner in crime. The two have gotten up to many antics in their ten years on the road together sharing Margaret's experiences. There may or may not be a story about a couple of tattoos in there . . .

MARGARET-OLEMAUN POKIAK-FENTON is best known as the indomitable subject of four award winning children's books about her time at residential school in the 1940s. She was born on Baille Island in the Arctic Ocean, en route with her nomadic family to their winter hunting grounds on Banks Island. Being Inuvialuk, her young childhood was filled with hunting trips by dogsled, and dangerous treks across the Arctic Ocean for supplies, in a schooner known as the *North Star*. At the age of eight, she traveled to Aklavik, a fur trading settlement founded by her great-grandfather, to attend the Catholic residential school there. Unlike most children, she begged to go to the residential school, despite the horrific reputation of such institutions. There was nothing she wanted more than to learn how to read. In her early twenties, while working for the Hudson's Bay Company in Tuktoyaktuk, she met her husband-to-be, Lyle, and followed him south to Fort St. John, BC, to become a cowboy's wife. Together, they raised eight children. Margaret is very active, speaking across Canada, sharing stories of resilience, the path to reclaiming cultural identity after residential school, and traditional Inuvialuit culture. She is a traditional language keeper, and is well known for her beadwork, embroidery, and bannock.

LIZ AMINI-HOLMES is a native San Franciscan and holds a BFA in Illustration from Academy of Art University and University of San Francisco. She's illustrated several books for children including *Fatty Legs: A True Story* and *A Stranger at Home* by Christy Jordan-Fenton and Margaret-Olemaun Pokiak-Fenton, *Chester Nez and The Unbreakable Code* by Joseph Bruchac, *Miracle* by Chanavia Haddock, and *The Fantastical Children of Pond Kingdom* by Ruth Finnegan. Liz's style is highly personalized and evocative as her art serves as a strong visual conduit to a story, creating a deeper story experience for the reader. Her work evokes magical realism by using rich, complex color and theatrical compositions. Her illustrations are often chosen to depict social advocacy for children and adults, multicultural awareness, and complex emotional topics, as well as folklore and mythology. Liz lives in the San Francisco Bay Area with her family and every growing menagerie of pets. When Liz is not illustrating she is working on a Masters in Art Therapy, teaching and obsessively reading and watching detective stories.